Disclaimer

All rights reserved - J.D. Simonson - Awakened Sways, LLC copyright 2023 ©
The information provided in this eBook, "Clear the Noise: Cultivate Mental Clarity for Success in Chaos," is for general informational purposes only. While every effort has been made to present accurate and up-to-date information, the author makes no representations or warranties of any kind, express or implied, about the completeness, accuracy, reliability, suitability, or availability of the content contained within.

The content of this eBook is based on the author's firsthand experiences, research, and knowledge in the field of mental clarity and personal development. It is not intended as a substitute for professional advice or guidance and should not be relied upon as such. Readers are encouraged to consult with qualified professionals for any specific concerns or questions they may have.

All rights reserved. No part of this book may be reproduced in any form or by any electronic or mechanical means, including information storage and retrieval systems, without written permission from the author, except for the use of brief quotations in a book review. It is illegal to copy this book, post it to a website, or distribute it by any other means without permission.

The author of this eBook is not responsible for any errors or omissions, or for any actions taken based on the information provided. They shall not be held liable for any loss or damages arising from the use of this eBook or any products, services, or techniques mentioned within.

Please use your own discretion when applying the concepts, techniques, or strategies discussed in this eBook. The reader assumes full responsibility for any risks involved and acknowledges that the author cannot be held accountable for any outcomes, positive or negative, resulting from the implementation of the information presented.

By accessing and using this eBook, you acknowledge and agree to the terms and conditions stated in this disclaimer.

Dedication to My Beautiful Wife

Table of Contents

Introduction..4

Chapter 1 - Understanding Mental Clutter & it's Triggers..........................9
The Impact of Negative Self-Talk.. 11
Conquering Worry and Anxiety... 13
Overcoming Fear and Insecurity... 15
Freeing Yourself from Guilt... 17
Dealing with Regret and Moving On... 19
Navigating the Influence of News and Media... 21
Achieving Financial Peace of Mind..23

Chapter 2 - Empowering the Present by Letting Go of the Past.............. 25
Recognizing the Importance of Letting Go...27
Breaking Free from the Victim Mentality..30
Harnessing the Power of Positive Affirmations..34
Embracing and Expressing Your Emotions.. 37
Finding Positivity in Past Experiences..40

Chapter 3 – Cultivating A Positive Mindset...42
Understanding the Brain's Relationship with Optimism 44
The Science of "You Are What You Think".. 46
Nurturing a Resilient and Positive Mindset.. 48

Chapter 4 - Gaining Mental Clarity Through Focus.................................. 53
Mastering the Art of Concentration.. 53
Identifying Factors that Distract Your Focus..55
Cultivating Productive Habits for Mental Clarity..59
Recognizing and Transforming Destructive Habits......................................63

Chapter 5 - Strategies for Clearing Mental Clutter & Unleashing Potential.....66
Practicing Mindfulness Techniques for Clarity...68
Harnessing the Power of Physical Exercise for Mental Well-being................70
Journaling and Effective Notetaking for Mental Organization...................... 73
Reading as a Gateway to Clarity and Growth.. 76
Creating and Utilizing Lists for Mental Organization....................................77
Minimizing Interruptions and Creating Mental Space.................................. 79
Overcoming Procrastination and Unlocking Productivity............................. 82

Conclusion.. 85

Introduction

"Welcome to 'Clear the Noise: Cultivate Mental Clarity for Success in Chaos.' Our minds possess immense possibilities and unlimited capabilities. However, in today's fast-paced and over-stimulated world, our minds often become overwhelmed, leaving us feeling restless and without inner peace.

The constant commotion within our minds never seems to cease, bombarding us with thoughts that breed anxiety, worry, and a sense of unease. We struggle to find focus, feeling disoriented and unable to break free from the rut that hinders our progress towards achieving our goals. These are all straightforward signs of a cluttered mind.

But fret not, for there are ways to train your brain to slow down, regain control of your thoughts, and find clarity amidst the chaos.

In this journey, we will explore the various aspects of mental clutter and provide you with practical strategies to clear the noise and attain the mental clarity necessary for success in a chaotic world.

The path to mental clarity begins with understanding the factors that contribute to a cluttered mind. One common obstacle is the baggage we carry from the past. We hold onto things that are beyond our control, harboring grudges, worries, and regrets that hinder our present and future.

To gain mental clarity, it is crucial to recognize the power of letting go, freeing ourselves from the burden of the past. True happiness awaits when we let go of the baggage from the past and embrace the power of positive thinking.

Another challenge to mental clarity is the constant, unremitting chatter that fills our minds. It deprives us of experiencing life's joys and impairs our cognitive abilities. This incessant chatter slows us down, clouds our decision-making, and leaves us feeling confused and absent-minded.

Learning to quiet this internal noise is essential for clearing the mind and gaining the clarity needed for success in both personal and professional endeavors.

Negative thoughts pose yet another obstacle to mental clarity. When allowed to persist, they become ingrained in our personality, influencing our thoughts and actions. Understanding the mechanisms of negative thought patterns is essential to break free from their grip and cultivate a positive mindset that fosters clarity, resilience, and growth.

Throughout this journey, we will explore a range of techniques and practices that empower you to clear the noise, declutter your mind, and achieve mental clarity.

From recognizing and addressing negative self-talk, worrying, and fear, to embracing positive affirmations, expressing emotions, and finding positivity in past experiences, each chapter will provide valuable insights and actionable strategies to support your path toward mental clarity and personal development.

Remember, gaining mental clarity is not a destination but an ongoing process. By implementing the techniques and principles shared in this guide, you will be equipped with the tools necessary to navigate the challenges of a chaotic world and thrive with a clear and focused mind.

The negative thoughts that often plague our minds have a profound impact on how we perceive ourselves and the world around us.

They create a barrier that prevents us from fully appreciating the blessings and simple joys that life has to offer.

Instead of counting our blessings, we find ourselves dwelling on our shortcomings, constantly complaining, and feeling discontented. But it does not have to be this way.

By embarking on a journey of cultivating mental clarity, you can break free from the grip of negative thoughts and create space for positive transformation. It is important to recognize that mental clutter not only affects our minds but can also manifest in physical symptoms, impacting our overall well-being.

To experience greater success and fulfillment, it is crucial to take intentional steps towards decluttering our minds and developing strategies for success. This involves letting go of the weight of the past, challenging negative thought patterns, and embracing a mindset that empowers us to overcome obstacles and seize opportunities.

Creating mental clarity is not a one-time event, but an ongoing process that requires commitment and practice. It involves cultivating self-awareness, mastering the art of positive thinking, and adopting effective strategies to maintain mental focus amidst the chaos of everyday life.

"True happiness awaits when we let go of the baggage from the past and embrace the power of positive thinking."

Chapter 1 - Understanding Mental Clutter & it's Triggers

To effectively address mental clutter and achieve mental clarity, it is important to understand the different types of mental clutter and how they manifest in our lives. By recognizing and identifying these types of mental clutter, you can take the necessary steps to overcome them and pave the way for greater success.

Negative Self-Talk: Constant self-criticism and negative internal dialogue that erode self-esteem and limit our potential. Worrying; Persistent and excessive worrying about future outcomes, leading to anxiety and distress.

Fear: Deep-seated fears that hinder us from taking risks, pursuing opportunities, and reaching our true potential.

Guilt: Lingering feelings of guilt and remorse from past actions or perceived shortcomings that hinder personal growth and happiness.

Regret: Dwelling on past decisions and experiences with a sense of remorse, preventing us from fully embracing the present and moving forward.

Throughout this chapter, we will explore each type of mental clutter, looking into their origins, consequences, and practical strategies to overcome them. Also go over some external types of clutter. By being aware of these strategies, you can declutter your mind, eliminate negative influences, and cultivate a mindset conducive to success.

The Impact of Negative Self-Talk

In our minds, a constant voice narrates our experiences and influences our perception of ourselves and the world around us. This internal dialogue guides our conversations, reveals our true desires, and shapes our self-esteem. This voice can be both positive and negative, with profound implications for our mental well-being.

Negative self-talk, a form of mental clutter, has a significant impact on our lives. When we convince ourselves that achieving a specific goal is impossible, we inadvertently set ourselves up for failure. The power of negative self-talk lies in its ability to create a toxic mental environment that permeates every aspect of our existence. Many individuals experience signs of negative mental clutter without fully realizing it.

Feelings of inadequacy, self-doubt, and a distorted self-image are common indicators of this detrimental internal dialogue. It is crucial to recognize these manifestations and acknowledge the widespread presence of this mental clutter.

The origins of negative self-talk can be traced back to various sources. It may arise from deeply ingrained beliefs, past experiences, or societal influences. Childhood conditioning, critical remarks from others, or the relentless pursuit of societal standards can contribute to the development of negative self-talk patterns.

These factors shape our perception of ourselves and perpetuate the cycle of self-criticism. The consequences of negative self-talk are profound and far-reaching. It diminishes our self-esteem, undermines our confidence, and restricts our potential for growth.

Negative self-talk breeds self-doubt, leading to indecisiveness and a fear of taking risks. It fosters a pessimistic mindset, making it challenging to find solutions to problems or recognize opportunities in difficult circumstances.

However, it is important to remember that negative self-talk is not an irreversible condition. By cultivating self-awareness and understanding its origins and consequences, we can begin to challenge and overcome this mental clutter. In subsequent sections, we will explore practical strategies to tackle negative self-talk and create a positive mental environment conducive to clarity and personal growth.

Conquering Worry and Anxiety

Worrying is another prevalent form of mental clutter that many individuals grapple with. While occasional worrying is a natural response to certain concerns, it can become chronic and overwhelming, consuming valuable mental space, and impeding our ability to find peace and clarity. For some, worrying becomes an ingrained habit, bordering on addiction or compulsion.

Chronic worriers often struggle to distinguish between situations within their control and those that are beyond their influence, leading to a cluttered and anxious mind. The uncertainty inherent in the future amplifies the hold that worrying has on our thoughts.

> "Not everything in life is predictable, but for some people, this fact can sometimes prove to be unbearable for them."

This quote highlights the challenge faced by individuals who find it difficult to cope with the unpredictability of life.

Worrying, fueled by anxieties beyond our control, exacerbates mental clutter, hindering our ability to maintain clarity and focus.

The consequences of chronic worrying are far-reaching. It drains our energy, heightens stress levels, and diminishes our overall well-being. Persistent worry prevents us from fully engaging in the present moment, as our minds become preoccupied with potential future scenarios and their associated anxieties.

However, it is crucial to recognize that we have the power to conquer worry and anxiety. By consciously shifting our focus towards more positive aspects of life, we can free ourselves from the grip of mental clutter. This requires cultivating mindfulness and redirecting our thoughts towards gratitude, self-care, and meaningful pursuits.

Overcoming Fear and Insecurity

Fear has a profound impact on our mental state, cluttering our minds and hindering effective information processing. When confronted with unfamiliar or challenging situations, the grip of fear can immobilize us, preventing us from taking necessary actions and impeding our progress.

It has the power to manipulate our thoughts and undermine our potential. "If you have ever experienced the feeling of dread in regard to a situation that you've never dealt with before, then you're aware of the fact that fear can stop you in your tracks."

This observation highlights the paralyzing effect of fear, which can sabotage our ability to navigate new experiences or pursue our goals. When fear takes hold of our minds, it becomes a formidable type of mental clutter that obstructs our path to growth and achievement.

Recognizing the impact of fear is essential for reclaiming control over our lives. If we allow fear to dominate our thoughts and prevent us from taking necessary steps toward our goals, it becomes evident that fear is a mental clutter that must be eliminated.

Overcoming fear and insecurity requires a deliberate and proactive approach. It involves acknowledging our fears, understanding their underlying causes, and developing strategies to confront and overcome them.

By cultivating self-awareness and practicing self-compassion, we can gradually dismantle the barriers that fear erects in our minds.

Freeing Yourself from Guilt

Guilt and shame have a profound influence on our mental state, often stemming from dissatisfaction with past decisions or actions that we regret. When these choices have negatively affected others or breached their trust, guilt and shame can consume a significant amount of mental space.

Holding onto these feelings can prevent us from moving forward and hinder our ability to let go of our poor choices.

"It becomes twofold when the choices that we've made in the past end up hurting people we care about or people who have trusted us in some way."

This acknowledgment emphasizes how guilt and shame intensify when our actions impact those we cherish or have a responsibility towards. The weight of guilt occupies our minds, hindering personal growth and tarnishing our self-worth, ultimately fostering low self-esteem.

Additionally, guilt and shame can function as gateways for negative self-talk. When we harbor guilt or shame over past situations, we may find ourselves growing resentful or angry towards ourselves.
These negative emotions pave the way for self-destructive thoughts to take hold, further cluttering our minds.

To reclaim mental clarity, it is crucial to acknowledge and confront feelings of guilt and shame. Recognizing these emotions within ourselves is the initial step towards freeing our minds from their grip. By embracing self-forgiveness and nurturing a positive relationship with our thoughts, we can gradually release the burden of guilt and shame.

Dealing with Regret and Moving On

Regret, the final type of mental clutter, poses a unique challenge for individuals seeking mental clarity. It is important to recognize that every person, regardless of their happiness and success, has experienced regret at some point in their lives.

Making decisions we later regret is an inevitable part of the human experience. However, what truly matters is how we navigate these decisions and their outcomes.

> **"It is not about the decision itself, but rather it is more about how you deal with the decision when the outcome isn't what you expected."**

Often, we tend to fixate on the outcome of a situation, dwelling on what went wrong, instead of embracing the valuable lessons learned from the experience. Being human entails the ability to objectively assess what transpired, identify areas for improvement, and cultivate an optimistic outlook for the future.

However, it is all too easy to become entangled in the past, allowing regret to overshadow our forward progress.

A common thread that connects all five types of mental clutter is the inability to let go. If you find yourself identifying with any of these forms of mental clutter, it is likely that you are occasionally too hard on yourself, creating barriers to achieving mental clarity.

Releasing yourself from the burden of past decisions and accepting that you could have chosen differently is paramount in your journey towards mental clarity.

> **"While it may be challenging, letting go of regret is an essential step on the path to mental clarity."**

Having explored the internal sources of mental clutter, it is crucial to acknowledge that external factors can also play a significant role in cluttering our minds and impeding mental clarity.

Two common triggers that often contribute to mental clutter are the influence of news and media, as well as financial concerns. Additionally, we will delve into the impact of dwelling on the past and the need to recognize and transform destructive habits.

Navigating the Influence of News and Media

The daily news has become a trigger point for many individuals, causing unnecessary worry, guilt, and stress. In today's world, it often feels like every news story focuses on violence, controversy, or negativity. If you find yourself regularly watching the nightly news, it is essential to assess whether it becomes a trigger for mental clutter in your life.

To determine the impact of the news on your mental well-being, consider keeping track of how you feel after watching it. You can write down your emotions or even use your phone to record your feelings. By taking note of the associated emotions, you gain a deeper understanding of the types of mental clutter that arise.

Once you have recorded your feelings, challenge yourself to take a few nights off from watching the news. Step away from the chaos and observe how you feel during this break.

You may be pleasantly surprised to find that your mind becomes clearer and more at ease when you refrain from consuming the constant stream of news.

Recognize that staying informed about current events is important but be mindful of how excessive exposure to negative news can clutter your mind and impact your overall well-being. It is crucial to strike a balance.

Avoiding the news altogether is not the solution, as being aware of global events is essential. However, by acknowledging the potential mental clutter caused by excessive news consumption, you can protect your mind when necessary.

Consider setting boundaries, such as limiting your news intake to specific times or seeking out more balanced and positive sources of information.

Achieving Financial Peace of Mind

Money is another trigger point that often leads to mental clutter for many individuals. Regardless of where you are in your career or financial journey, money can evoke feelings of fear, worry, and regret.

The constant thoughts about money and how to acquire more of it can consume your mind and hinder your mental clarity. Fortunately, there are strategies you can employ to alleviate this mental burden.

One effective approach is to shift your mindset regarding money. Instead of fixating on the lack of money or feeling anxious about it, cultivate a sense of gratitude for the money you do have. Appreciating what you currently possess helps create a positive and abundant mindset, reducing the mental clutter associated with money-related worries.

Another crucial step is to be honest with yourself about your financial situation. Take the time to evaluate where your money is going and identify areas where you can cut costs. This self-awareness allows you to make conscious decisions about your spending habits and prioritize what truly matters to you.

By proactively managing your finances, you gain a sense of control and minimize the mental clutter caused by financial concerns.

Shift your focus from obsessing over money to cultivating gratitude for what you have and take control of your finances to reduce mental clutter and achieve financial peace of mind.

Chapter 2 - Empowering the Present by Letting Go of the Past

The past can exert a major influence on our minds, especially when it comes to our interactions with others. We all carry experiences from the past that we would rather forget, and these memories can create mental clutter and hinder our ability to move forward.

However, it is essential to recognize the importance of letting go and healing from past wounds to regain mental clarity.

Life is full of difficulties, and sometimes we are left with emotional scars as a result. It is crucial to acknowledge and address these scars in the most compassionate and nurturing way possible.

By actively working on healing ourselves, we can release the grip of the past and prevent it from dictating our responses to future situations. Letting go of the past is a powerful practice because it allows us to free ourselves from the burdens and negative emotions associated with past experiences. When we hold onto the past, it becomes a lens through which we view the world, distorting our perceptions and limiting our ability to fully engage in the present.

Releasing the Grip of the Past

Another trigger that leads to mental clutter for many of us in the past. Sometimes the past is simply a reference point as we move through life. However, this does not mean that we should allow the past to define our future.

When you focus on the past, it can seem like your inner demons shine brighter than they should. We have all made mistakes, taken others for granted, and have done things of which we are not proud.

When you focus on these negative aspects of your past, rather than the positive ones, you are more likely to be overly hard on yourself.

If you can start to think of the past as being less defining to who you are today, it can lead to a less cluttered mind when you are making important decisions.

Recognizing the Importance of Letting Go

In our journey through life, we often encounter situations where we have been hurt by others, leaving emotional scars that linger in our minds. These experiences can lead to a general sense of distrust, causing us to hold onto past pain and preventing us from forming positive relationships with others. This emotional baggage becomes a form of mental clutter that influences how we live our lives.

Understanding the significance of letting go is the first step in freeing ourselves from the grip of the past. Rather than viewing it as a daunting task, we can reframe letting go as a positive act of self-care and personal growth.

By doing so, we open ourselves up to a range of possibilities for healing and transformation. Here are some key aspects to consider when embarking on the journey of letting go:

Releases You of a Burden

Carrying the weight of past hurts is emotionally exhausting. By forgiving the circumstances and letting go of the pain caused by those situations, we lighten the load on our psyche. Releasing the burden allows us to reclaim our energy and focus on nurturing our well-being.

Releases You of Resentment

Letting go does not necessarily mean reconciling with the person who hurt us. Instead, it involves freeing ourselves from the emotional burden of resentment, sadness, anger, and pain. By shifting our focus away from the other person and onto our own healing, we become better versions of ourselves, unencumbered by negative emotions.

Brings You More Understanding

It is important to recognize that those who have caused us pain may be hurting themselves. Cultivating compassion for others, even in difficult circumstances, can make it easier for us to let go of the past. Understanding that everyone is navigating their own struggles allows us to find empathy and move forward with greater peace.

Requires You to Forgive Yourself

When we hold onto the past, we may also blame ourselves for the circumstances that unfolded. It is vital to extend compassion to ourselves, acknowledging that relationships are complex, and we may bear some responsibility along with being a victim.

Forgiving ourselves allows us to release self-judgment and create space for personal growth and transformation. Letting go of the past is a powerful act of self-liberation. It enables us to release emotional clutter, heal our wounds, and cultivate inner peace.

Breaking Free from the Victim Mentality

We all encounter situations where others have hurt us, and it is essential to acknowledge that their actions were their own choices. Similarly, how we choose to respond and dwell on those experiences is also within our control.

To truly let go of the past, we must recognize when we are placing ourselves in the role of the victim. Playing the victim is a manifestation of weakness that allows the person who caused us pain to retain power over us, even long after the event has occurred.

It keeps us trapped in a cycle of negativity, preventing us from moving forward and embracing a more empowered mindset. Instead of perpetuating this victimhood, it is time to reclaim our agency and shift our perspective. Allow me to share a story that illustrates a paradigm shift from victimhood to empowerment:

Jason was a hardworking and ambitious individual who had always strived for success in his career.
He had invested countless hours and made numerous sacrifices to climb the corporate ladder.

However, despite his best efforts, he faced setback after setback, leading to feelings of frustration and resentment. One day, while scrolling through social media, Jason came across a post by an old colleague, Sarah. Sarah had started her own successful business and seemed to be living a life of fulfillment and accomplishment. Seeing her achievements triggered a wave of envy and self-doubt within Jason.

He could not help but compare himself to her and wonder why he had not achieved the same level of success. Feeling overwhelmed by negative emotions, Jason sought guidance from a mentor who had overcome similar challenges in his own life. The mentor shared a personal story that resonated deeply with Jason. He told Jason about a time when he too had experienced setbacks and feelings of inadequacy.

The mentor explained that dwelling on comparisons and past failures only served to clutter the mind with negativity, preventing growth and progress. He emphasized the importance of focusing on one's own journey, strengths, and unique path to success.

The mentor encouraged Jason to let go of the past and shift his mindset towards gratitude and self-empowerment. Inspired by the mentor's story and advice, Jason decided to make a paradigm shift in his thinking. He recognized that constantly comparing himself to others and fixating on past failures only hindered his own progress.

Instead, he chose to focus on his own accomplishments, no matter how small, and to be grateful for the lessons he had learned along the way. With a newfound perspective, Jason began to invest his energy in personal growth and self-improvement. He enrolled in courses and attended workshops to enhance his skills and knowledge. He sought out new opportunities and collaborations that aligned with his passions and values. Most importantly, he learned to celebrate his own achievements, no matter how insignificant they may have seemed in comparison to others.

Over time, Jason's mindset shift and renewed focus on personal growth paid off. He began to see positive changes in his career and personal life. By letting go of comparison and embracing his own unique journey, Jason found a sense of clarity, purpose, and fulfillment that had eluded him before.

Jason's story reminds us of the power of letting go of comparisons and past failures. It teaches us that true success comes from embracing our own journey, recognizing our strengths, and pursuing our passions with authenticity and gratitude. By releasing the mental clutter of comparison, we create space for personal growth, self-acceptance, and a greater sense of fulfillment in our lives.

As we continue with the upcoming sections, we will explore practical strategies and techniques to help you release the burden of comparison and past failures, enabling you to embrace your own unique path and create a life of purpose, contentment, and personal success.

Harnessing the Power of Positive Affirmations

Now that you have realized that you are in control and have started to shift your focus to the present, it is essential to work on rebuilding your self-esteem in order to let go of the past once and for all. Dwelling on adverse events from the past can have a negative impact on your self-confidence over time.

To counteract this, incorporating positive affirmations into your daily routine can be immensely powerful. Positive affirmations are statements that reinforce positive beliefs about yourself and your abilities. By repeating these affirmations regularly, you can retrain your mind to see yourself as deserving of success and create a positive internal dialogue.

Here are some examples of powerful affirmations that express mental clarity and empowerment:

"I am in control of my thoughts and emotions, and I choose to focus on positivity and clarity in every aspect of my life."

"I release the past and embrace the present moment with an open heart and a clear mind."

"I am worthy of success, happiness, and abundance, and I am fully capable of achieving my goals."

"I trust in my own abilities and have confidence in my decision-making."

"I let go of self-doubt and embrace my inner strength and resilience."

"I am deserving of love, respect, and all the good things that life has to offer."

"I attract positive experiences and opportunities that align with my highest good."

"I am capable of learning from my past experiences and using them as steppingstones for personal growth and success."

"I release all negative self-perceptions and replace them with empowering beliefs about myself."

"I am enough, and I have the power to create the life I desire."

Remember, the key to harnessing the power of positive affirmations is consistency. Repeat these affirmations daily, preferably in front of a mirror or in a quiet space where you can fully absorb their meaning.

Embrace them with conviction and allow them to gradually reshape your self-image and mindset.

With time and practice, positive affirmations can help you build mental clarity, boost your self-esteem, and let go of the past, empowering you to create a brighter and more fulfilling future.

Embracing and Expressing Your Emotions

When we suppress our emotions and keep the problems from the past bottled up, they do not simply disappear. Instead, they linger in our minds, occupying valuable mental space. This can lead to a cycle of creating scenarios and playing the 'what if' game because we never expressed our true feelings to the person who caused us harm in the past.

We begin to wonder what might have happened if we had spoken up or confronted the situation head-on. To break free from the habit of playing the 'what if' game, it is essential to become more open about our emotions and express them honestly when we experience them.

By doing so, we not only relieve our minds of anxious thoughts but also reduce resentment towards the situations we have encountered. Here are three examples of the 'what if' game and how it can affect us:

Example 1: The Missed Opportunity

You remember a time when you had the chance to pursue a passion or take an exciting opportunity, but fear or self-doubt held you back. Now, you find yourself wondering, "What if I had taken that opportunity? How different would my life be?"

These 'what if' scenarios can keep you stuck in a loop of regret and prevent you from fully embracing new opportunities in the present.

Example 2: The Unspoken Words

There is someone in your life who hurt you deeply, but you never expressed your true feelings to them. You find yourself replaying the situation in your mind and imagining what might have happened if you had confronted them or expressed your pain.

The 'what if' game in this context can fuel anger, resentment, and a sense of powerlessness, preventing you from moving forward and finding closure.

Example 3: The Past Relationship

You think about a past romantic relationship that ended, and you wonder, "What if we had worked things out? Could we have had a future together?" This line of thinking keeps you anchored in the past and prevents you from fully embracing new possibilities and relationships in the present.

The 'what if' scenarios can lead to longing, dissatisfaction, and difficulty in moving on.

To break free from the 'what if' game, it is important to acknowledge and express your emotions in a healthy and constructive way. Practice open and honest communication with yourself and others. Share your feelings, concerns, and desires with trusted friends, family, or a therapist.

By expressing your emotions, you release the mental burden of the 'what if' scenarios and create space for healing, growth, and new possibilities in your life.

Finding Positivity in Past Experiences

To truly let go of the past, it is crucial to shift our perspective and reframe our relationship with it. Instead of solely focusing on the negative aspects that have led us to our current situations, we must also seek out and acknowledge the positive elements that have emerged from our past experiences.

Take the time to reflect on the good times, the moments of joy, the lessons learned, and the personal growth that has come from your past. By consciously reminding yourself of these positive aspects, you allow your mind to clear out the lingering negativity associated with past events.

It is important to understand that letting go of the past is the key to moving forward and attaining mental clarity. Holding onto grudges, resentments, and self-blame for past wrongs and mistakes can hinder our progress and prevent us from realizing our full potential.

By embracing the positive aspects of our past experiences, we can gain a new perspective on the lessons learned and use them as steppingstones for personal growth.

Recognizing the strength, resilience, and wisdom we have gained from challenging situations empowers us to move forward with confidence and clarity.

Moreover, finding positivity in past experiences allows us to cultivate gratitude and appreciation for the journey we have traveled. It helps us recognize the resilience of the human spirit and the transformative power of overcoming obstacles.

As you let go of the negative aspects of the past and focus on the positive, you create space for new opportunities, fresh perspectives, and personal evolution.

By embracing the lessons and growth from the past, you can channel your energy towards creating a brighter and more fulfilling future.

Chapter 3 – Cultivating A Positive Mindset

Developing a positive mindset goes beyond simply feeling happier or having an optimistic outlook. While these are natural by-products of positive thinking, there are numerous benefits that can significantly enhance your mental clarity and contribute to greater success.

Recent studies have shown that positive thinking is linked to your brain's reward system and pleasure stimulus.

When you engage in positive thinking and experience the pleasure and happiness it brings, your brain's reward system is activated, reinforcing this pattern, and encouraging more positive thinking.

Positive thinking has a snowball effect on the brain. Once you start thinking positively, your mind craves more of those positive feelings, leading to a continuous cycle of positive thinking. As a result, your interactions with others and your general outlook on life become more optimistic.

Understanding the Brain's Relationship with Optimism

Positive thinking has a profound impact on the growth and development of the brain, as supported by scientific research. Specifically, positive thinking has been found to stimulate the growth of neural connections in the brain, enhancing its overall functioning.

Even if you are not naturally inclined towards positive thinking, neural connections will still develop in your brain. However, when you actively engage in positive thinking, these connections grow at a faster rate.

This becomes particularly significant as you age, as the brain's ability to form new connections naturally slows down. By cultivating a positive mindset, you can extend the efficiency and effectiveness of your brain's functioning.

Positive thinking offers two additional benefits in terms of cognitive output and analysis. When you think positively, your mind becomes more adept at processing thoughts rapidly, leading to improved cognitive agility.

Positive thinking enhances alertness, allowing you to stay more focused and engaged in various tasks. In addition, positive thinking facilitates problem-solving by enabling more efficient and effective solutions. Negative thoughts often limit our thinking to pessimistic outcomes, narrowing our perspective.

On the other hand, positive thinking encourages openness to diverse possibilities and broadens our range of solutions. By embracing a positive mindset, our brains can explore a wider array of scenarios, ultimately leading to more creative and effective problem-solving.

Understanding the profound relationship between positive thinking and the brain, we can recognize the significance of cultivating optimism. Positive thinking not only stimulates the growth of neural connections but also enhances thought processing, alertness, and problem-solving abilities.

By actively engaging in positive thinking, we open ourselves up to a world of possibilities and empower our minds to navigate life's challenges with clarity and creativity.

The Science of "You Are What You Think"

The power of positive thinking goes beyond just influencing the brain; it also has a profound impact on our actions and life's outcomes. Our thoughts serve as powerful precursors to the decisions we make and the actions we take—or do not take. By understanding this connection, we can better appreciate the role of positive thinking in decluttering our minds and shaping our lives.

Positive thinkers perceive the world as a place full of opportunities and possibilities. They see themselves as capable of achieving their desires and goals. This optimistic outlook becomes a platform for them to take courageous leaps towards their dreams.

Positive thinkers embrace challenges as steppingstones to growth and success. On the contrary, negative thinking fosters a belief that our current circumstances define our future, leaving little room for improvement. When people adopt a negative mindset, they become trapped in a cycle of self-limiting thoughts.

These negative thoughts hinder personal growth and prevent individuals from reaching their full potential. It is crucial to understand that life is constantly evolving, and so are we as individuals.

Embracing change and growth is fundamental to our human experience. Succumbing to negative thinking can stifle personal development, inhibiting us from discovering our true capabilities.

This is where positive thinking emerges as a pivotal force. By cultivating positive thoughts, we empower ourselves to transcend limitations and overcome challenges. Positive thoughts serve as catalysts for personal growth, propelling us towards realizing our aspirations and ambitions.

It is incredibly important to recognize that our thoughts hold immense power. We become what we consistently think. Positive thoughts align us with success and fulfillment, while negative thoughts restrain us from reaching our potential.

Therefore, mastering the art of positive thinking is not just a mere exercise; it is a transformative journey that allows us to create the life we envision and deserve.

Nurturing a Resilient and Positive Mindset

Now that the significance of positive thinking for your success is evident, let us explore how you can cultivate a more positive outlook on life. While some individuals may naturally possess a greater sense of positivity, it does not mean that you cannot develop and nurture this mindset within yourself.

Primarily, it's essential to understand that being optimistic doesn't always translate to being blindly positive. Optimistic individuals acknowledge that excessive positivity can sometimes be counterproductive to their well-being and mental clarity.

Instead, positive thinkers are individuals who can perceive both the positive and negative aspects of any given situation. They possess the ability to acknowledge challenges and obstacles realistically. However, when faced with adversity, they consciously choose to focus on the positive elements, allowing them to maintain hope and a sense of possibility.

Finding this balance between optimism and realism is crucial, especially if you tend to grapple with more negative thoughts than positive ones. It does not mean suppressing negative emotions or denying the existence of challenges; instead, it is about recognizing them while actively directing your focus towards constructive and optimistic perspectives.

Rather than attempting to be excessively optimistic all the time, a more practical approach is to train yourself to evaluate situations with a holistic mindset. Acknowledge both the positive and negative aspects, and then consciously shift your focus towards the positive aspects. This shift in focus can significantly impact your overall outlook on life and the way you oversee various circumstances.

Incorporating this balanced approach to positive thinking allows you to build resilience and cope better with life's difficulties. By acknowledging challenges while maintaining a positive perspective, you become better equipped to navigate through difficulties and pursue your goals with a determined spirit.

It is about cultivating a healthier thought pattern that will help you embrace life's uncertainties with optimism and a willingness to grow. In addition to understanding the importance of positive thinking and adopting a balanced perspective, there are practical strategies you can implement to nurture a positive mindset. Here are a few suggestions:

Volunteer Your Time

Engaging in volunteer work can be a powerful way to foster positivity. By dedicating your time and energy to helping others, you not only make a positive impact on their lives but also experience a sense of fulfillment and purpose.

Choose causes or organizations that resonate with your interests and values, and actively contribute to making a difference in your community.

Keep a Gratitude Journal

If volunteering is not your preferred method, consider keeping a gratitude journal. Set aside a few moments each day, either before bed or in the morning, to reflect on and write down the things for which you are grateful.

Focus on the present day or the previous day, noting the positive aspects, achievements, or moments of joy you experienced. This practice trains your mind to shift its focus towards the positive aspects of your life, helping you cultivate a sense of gratitude and appreciation.

Practice Random Acts of Kindness

Another effective way to shift your mindset from negative to positive is by incorporating acts of kindness into your daily life. Take the initiative to be kinder and more compassionate towards those around you. This can involve small gestures such as offering a genuine compliment, lending a helping hand, or actively listening to someone who needs support.

By spreading kindness, you not only improve your relationships and create a positive environment, but you also encourage a positive mindset within yourself.

Engage in Mindfulness and Meditation

Mindfulness and meditation practices are powerful tools for cultivating a positive mindset. Set aside dedicated time each day to engage in mindfulness exercises or meditation. These practices help you become more present, observe your thoughts without judgment, and cultivate a state of calm and clarity.
With consistent practice, you can train your mind to focus on the present moment, reduce negativity, and enhance your overall well-being.

Surround Yourself with Positive Influences

Take a closer look at the people you interact with and the media you consume. Surround yourself with positive influences that uplift and inspire you. Seek out supportive and optimistic individuals who share similar goals and values. Limit your exposure to negative news, social media, or any content that consistently brings you down. By curating a positive environment, you create space for personal growth, increased motivation, and a more positive mindset.

Chapter 4 - Gaining Mental Clarity Through Focus

Along with learning how to think positively, another way you can limit the amount of mental clutter in your head and regain control of your mind is by improving your focus. There are a number of external factors that can lead you to lack focus and some ways to help you focus better and more consistently.

Mastering the Art of Concentration

Why Focus is Important?

The ability to concentrate is an invaluable skill that every successful individual must cultivate to some extent. When you develop strong focus, you unlock several mental capabilities that can significantly contribute to your achievements:

1. Setting Aligned Goals: With enhanced focus, you can set goals that align with your preferences and desires. By eliminating distractions and honing in on what truly matters to you, you gain clarity in defining your aspirations and objectives.

2. Making Confident Choices: Improved focus empowers you to make choices with greater certainty. By understanding your goals and aligning your decisions accordingly, you can confidently navigate through life's opportunities and challenges.

3. Charting Your Path: Concentration allows you to discern the path that leads to your desired outcomes. By minimizing mental clutter and distractions, you can focus on the necessary steps and strategies that will guide you toward your goals.

4. Cultivating Motivation: When your focus is sharpened, you find increased motivation in your daily tasks. With a clear understanding of how each activity contributes to your larger objectives, you can approach your work with drive, confidence, and enthusiasm.

Identifying Factors that Distract Your Focus

To clear your mind of mental clutter and regain clarity, it is important to identify the factors that hinder your focus. If you find yourself frequently losing concentration or being labeled as a "scatterbrain," there may be underlying causes beyond a simple inability to stay organized.

Recognizing these factors and understanding their impact on your focus is crucial for addressing the root issues. Here are some steps to help you identify distractions and stressors that may be affecting your ability to concentrate:

Reflect on Your Patterns

Take time to reflect on your past experiences and patterns of distraction. Consider situations where you have struggled to maintain focus. Are there specific tasks, environments, or circumstances that consistently lead to distractions? Look for commonalities and recurring themes that may provide insights into the factors that disrupt your concentration.

For example, you may notice that you lose focus when there are noise distractions, or that certain types of tasks require more mental effort, causing you to become easily distracted.

External Distractions

Assess the external distractions in your surroundings. Pay attention to the physical environment in which you work or study. Are there noises, interruptions, or visual stimuli that pull your attention away from the task at hand?

It could be loud conversations, phone notifications, cluttered workspace, or social media temptations. Identify these external distractions and think about strategies to minimize or eliminate them. This could involve finding a quieter workspace, turning off notifications, organizing your physical space, or using website blockers to limit access to distracting websites.

Internal Distractions

Explore the internal factors that contribute to your lack of focus. Internal distractions can include stress, anxiety, negative thoughts, or emotional turmoil. Take a moment to assess your mental and emotional state when you struggle to concentrate. Are there specific worries, concerns, or unresolved issues that occupy your mind?

These internal distractions can be equally disruptive to your focus. Consider techniques such as mindfulness meditation, deep breathing exercises, or journaling to help manage these internal distractions and create a calmer mental state.

Overwhelm and Multitasking

Examine your workload and commitments. Are you taking on too many tasks simultaneously? Trying to multitask can fragment your attention and lead to decreased focus. Identify areas where you may be overcommitting or spreading yourself too thin. Learn to prioritize tasks and allocate dedicated time for each one, allowing you to focus fully on one task at a time. By reducing overwhelm and avoiding multitasking, you can enhance your ability to concentrate.

Emotional Well-being

Your emotional well-being plays a significant role in your ability to focus. Negative emotions, such as stress, anxiety, or even boredom, can diminish your concentration. Assess how your emotional state affects your focus and overall mental clarity.

Practice self-care activities that promote emotional well-being, such as exercise, adequate sleep, hobbies, and spending time with loved ones. Engaging in activities that bring you joy, and relaxation can create a positive mindset and enhance your focus.

Time Management

Poor time management can lead to a lack of focus and productivity. Evaluate how you manage your time and whether you are allocating sufficient time for important tasks. Procrastination or constant rushing can create unnecessary stress and distractions. Adopt effective time management techniques, such as prioritizing tasks, breaking them into smaller manageable chunks, setting realistic deadlines, and creating a structured schedule.

By managing your time effectively, you can reduce the mental clutter associated with feeling overwhelmed and gain better control of your focus. Remember, identifying the factors that distract your focus is an ongoing process of self-reflection and awareness.

Continuously monitor your environment, emotions, and habits to pinpoint areas where improvements can be made. By addressing these factors, you can create a conducive mental space that supports enhanced focus and mental clarity.

Cultivating Productive Habits for Mental Clarity

In addition to external factors and habits that contribute to a lack of focus, certain lifestyle choices and habits can also impact your mental clarity. By cultivating productive habits, you can optimize your brain's functioning and enhance your ability to concentrate. Here are some habits to consider:

Balanced Sugar Intake

Overeating sugar can have detrimental effects on your physical health and cognitive function. Studies have linked excessive sugar consumption to increased risks of obesity, diabetes, and even Alzheimer's disease.

To maintain mental clarity, aim for a balanced sugar intake by reducing your consumption of processed sugars and opting for healthier alternatives. Focus on whole foods and incorporate natural sugars from fruits to satisfy your sweet cravings without the negative impact on mental function.

Adequate Fat Consumption

Your brain relies on healthy fats for optimal function, as a huge portion of the brain is composed of fat. Consuming insufficient healthy fats can impair cognitive abilities and hinder mental clarity. Incorporate sources of good fats, such as avocados, nuts, seeds, and fatty fish, into your diet. These fats provide essential nutrients for brain health and support the production of necessary chemicals for optimal brain function.

Hydration

Dehydration can negatively affect cognitive performance and impair focus. Make it a habit to drink an adequate amount of water throughout the day to keep your brain hydrated. Aim for at least eight glasses of water daily and adjust your intake based on your activity level and environment. Staying properly hydrated helps optimize brain function, enhances mental clarity, and reduces mental fatigue.

Essential Minerals

Essential minerals like vitamin D and vitamin B12 play a crucial role in brain health and cognitive function. Vitamin B12 supports memory and digestive health, while vitamin D is associated with mood improvement and combating depressive states. Ensure you are getting sufficient levels of these vitamins through a balanced diet or supplements.

Consult with a healthcare professional to determine the appropriate dosage and sources of these essential minerals.

You can absorb Vitamin D through your skin from the sun. It is known to improve mood and has been linked to improving depressive states. If you can clear your mind by just taking a multivitamin daily, why wouldn't you?

Mindful Eating

Practicing mindful eating can help you develop a healthier relationship with food and improve mental clarity. Take the time to savor and fully experience each meal, paying attention to the tastes, textures, and nourishment it provides.

Avoid distractions such as screens or work while eating, as this can hinder your ability to focus on the present moment and fully enjoy your meal. By practicing mindful eating, you can enhance your overall well-being, including mental clarity and focus.

Regular Exercise

Engaging in regular physical exercise has numerous benefits for your mental clarity. Exercise increases blood flow to the brain, releases endorphins, and promotes overall brain health. Aim for at least 30 minutes of moderate intensity exercise most days of the week. Find activities that you enjoy, such as walking, jogging, dancing, or yoga, and incorporate them into your routine to support mental clarity and overall well-being.

There are a lot of factors that contribute to mental clutter and the brain's ability or inability to focus on a single task or thought at a time. This includes how you fuel your body and mind and keep it energized.

While writing down your thoughts can help you to slow your thoughts down and eliminate some of the mental clutter taking up space in your mind, you also must take care of your body and provide it with the fuel that it needs to function correctly.

Recognizing and Transforming Destructive Habits

Gaining mental clarity requires recognizing and transforming destructive habits that may be contributing to mental clutter and hindering personal growth. It is common to feel stuck in certain patterns, believing that circumstances cannot be changed. However, breaking free from these limitations is an essential step toward decluttering the mind and achieving mental clarity.

Start by engaging in self-reflection to examine your current attitudes and beliefs. If you find yourself trapped in a mindset that resists change, acknowledge it as a barrier to mental clarity.

Embrace the understanding that change is possible and that you hold the power to transform your circumstances.
Next, assess your associations. Take a close look at the people you surround yourself with, including friends, family, and colleagues. Evaluate whether these relationships contribute positively to your life or if they foster negative thinking and mental clutter.

Surrounding yourself with individuals who inspire and motivate you can significantly impact your mindset and help cultivate a more positive outlook. If necessary, be prepared to make changes to your social circle, aligning it with your personal growth and clarity goals.

Another crucial aspect to consider is the impact of material possessions on your mental state. Physical clutter often translates into mental clutter, making it difficult to focus and think clearly. Evaluate your physical environment and declutter spaces that have become overwhelmed with unnecessary items.

Take the time to organize your living and working areas, creating an environment that promotes mental clarity. Donate or discard possessions that no longer serve a purpose or bring you joy, freeing up space both physically and mentally.

Additionally, evaluate your job satisfaction. The nature of your work significantly influences your overall well-being and mental clarity. If you find yourself feeling unfulfilled, stressed, or stuck in a job that does not align with your values or passions, it is crucial to address this issue.

Explore alternative career opportunities, consider pursuing further education or training, or explore possibilities for growth within your current job.

Taking proactive steps to improve job satisfaction will have a profound impact on your mental clarity and overall happiness.

To initiate change, create a well-structured plan of action. Break down your goals into smaller, manageable steps, and establish a realistic timeline for achieving them.

Embrace flexibility and adapt your plan as needed. Commitment to transforming destructive habits and making positive changes will help you clear your mind of clutter and gain mental clarity. Remember that the process of recognizing and transforming destructive habits takes time and effort. Embrace patience and perseverance, seeking support from trusted individuals or professionals when needed.

Celebrate each small step forward, as each one brings you closer to a clearer mind, improved focus, and greater success in various aspects of your life. By actively working to recognize and transform destructive habits, you pave the way for personal growth and the attainment of mental clarity.

Chapter 5 - Strategies for Clearing Mental Clutter & Unleashing Potential

In the pursuit of mental clarity and unleashing our full potential, it is essential to incorporate daily practices that aid in clearing out mental clutter. These practices can provide us with effective tools to regain control over our thoughts and overcome feelings of overwhelm.

By implementing small actions consistently, we create a framework to navigate challenging situations and foster a more positive and focused mindset. These strategies serve as a compass to guide us when confronted with unhelpful thoughts that impede our progress.

They offer practical steps to declutter our minds and create space for innovative ideas, insights, and possibilities. By engaging in these practices regularly, we can nurture a clearer, more purposeful state of mind that propels us towards greater success.

In the following sections, we will explore various strategies and techniques that can aid in clearing mental clutter and unleashing our potential. These strategies can be customized to fit individual preferences and can be seamlessly integrated into daily routines. By adopting these small but powerful actions, we empower ourselves to navigate challenges, enhance focus, and tap into our true capabilities.

Practicing Mindfulness Techniques for Clarity

In moments of overwhelm or when experiencing a lack of focus, incorporating mindfulness techniques can be immensely helpful in regaining composure and mental clarity.

One such technique is mindful breathing, which can effectively calm the heart and clear the mind. When negative or overwhelming thoughts begin to bombard your mind, find a quiet space, close your eyes, and repeat the following mental cues: "inhale" as you take a slow, deep breath, and "exhale" as you release the breath gradually.

Engaging in intentional, deep breathing allows you to slow down and regain a sense of control over your thoughts and emotions. Scientific research has shown that deep breathing can lower stress levels and even reduce blood pressure. By focusing on your breath, you bring your attention to the present moment and create a mental space where other thoughts can take a backseat.

Mindful breathing serves as an anchor, redirecting your focus away from the clutter of competing thoughts and toward the sensations of each breath. By noticing and observing the rhythm of your breathing, you create an opportunity to detach from racing thoughts and cultivate a state of inner calm and clarity.

Incorporating mindful breathing into your daily routine can provide a moment of respite amidst the chaos of everyday life. It is a simple yet powerful tool that can be accessed anytime, anywhere, allowing you to regain your footing and approach challenges with renewed focus and mental clarity.

Harnessing the Power of Physical Exercise for Mental Well-being

Incorporating physical exercise into your daily routine can be a powerful method to clear your mind of clutter and promote mental well-being. Engaging in regular exercise not only directs your focus towards the physical activity at hand but also brings about significant positive changes in your brain, supported by scientific evidence.

When you exercise, your brain releases endorphins, often referred to as "feel-good" chemicals.

These endorphins contribute to a sense of calmness and relaxation, helping to alleviate stress and anxiety. Moreover, regular physical activity offers a multitude of benefits for mental well-being:
Increasing self-esteem

Regular exercise can boost your self-esteem and confidence. Achieving fitness goals, improving physical strength and endurance, and taking care of your body can enhance your perception of self-worth.

Easing symptoms of anxiety and depression

Exercise has been shown to be an effective natural remedy for managing symptoms of anxiety and depression. Physical activity promotes the release of neurotransmitters like serotonin and dopamine, which are associated with improved mood and reduced feelings of anxiety.

Improving sleep

Engaging in exercise can promote better sleep quality. Physical activity helps regulate the sleep-wake cycle, making it easier to fall asleep and experience restful sleep. Adequate sleep further contributes to mental clarity and overall well-being.

Providing a sense of control

Incorporating exercise into your daily routine allows you to take control of your physical health. This sense of control extends to your mental well-being, as engaging in regular exercise fosters discipline, consistency, and a proactive approach to self-care.

Enhancing mood and increasing optimism

Physical activity stimulates the release of endorphins and other mood-enhancing neurotransmitters, leading to an improved mood and increased optimism. Regular exercise can leave you feeling energized, positive, and ready to tackle challenges.

If you are currently not engaged in much physical activity, starting with small steps can have a profound impact on your mental clarity. Incorporate exercise into your daily routine by taking evening walks, participating in yoga or other low-impact activities, or exploring activities that bring you joy and movement.

Journaling and Effective Notetaking for Mental Organization

Journaling and effective notetaking are powerful techniques to train your brain to slow down, declutter your mind, and gain mental clarity. It does not require a formal journaling process; instead, it involves performing a "brain dump" using whatever writing utensils are available to you.

By regularly transferring the multitude of ideas swirling in your mind onto paper, you can establish positive habits that lead to lasting change in your mental organization and focus.

Many individuals experience a sense of relief after writing down their thoughts, as if the weight of their brain's activities has been purged from their mind. This process helps to clear mental clutter and provides an opportunity to acknowledge and release thoughts that may be occupying your mind unnecessarily. To make the most of journaling and note-taking for mental organization, consider jotting down the following:

The steps to accomplish your goals;

Break down your goals into manageable steps and record them in your journal. This act of writing helps to reinforce your commitment and provides a clear roadmap for achieving your aspirations.

A list of current worries

Identify and write down the worries and concerns that are preoccupying your mind. Externalizing these thoughts allows you to gain perspective and develop strategies for addressing them effectively.

Details about relationships

If a particular relationship is straining your mental energy, write down your thoughts and feelings about it. Journaling can help you process emotions, gain insights into the situation, and identify potential resolutions.

Daily reflections

Take a few moments each day to jot down reflections on your experiences, emotions, and achievements. This practice fosters self-awareness and personal growth.

The beauty of journaling and note-taking lies in its flexibility; there are no rigid rules about what you should or should not write. The primary goal is to clear mental clutter by transferring thoughts from your mind onto paper, allowing you to acknowledge, analyze, and release them.

Consistency is key in developing this practice. Set aside dedicated moments each day to engage in journaling or note-taking. Over time, you will find that these habits create a space for mental clarity, reducing the overwhelm of constant mental chatter, and empowering you to navigate life's challenges with greater focus and composure.

Reading as a Gateway to Clarity and Growth

Reading is a powerful tool for decluttering the mind and fostering personal growth. An enjoyable book offers an escape from reality that is unique and enriching, providing an experience that other forms of entertainment like movies or television shows may not fully replicate.

Unlike passive entertainment, reading requires active engagement from the mind. It encourages deep thinking, imagination, and critical analysis. As you immerse yourself in a compelling book, your mind works actively to process the details, characters, and ideas presented within the pages.

The act of reading not only transports you to different worlds but also allows you to explore diverse perspectives, challenging your existing beliefs and expanding your understanding of the world.

Creating and Utilizing Lists for Mental Organization

Taking a few moments before bedtime to jot down the tasks occupying your mind can be remarkably beneficial.

There are numerous ways to maintain such a list: you can use a traditional pen and paper, a digital note-taking app, or one of the many task management apps available for smartphones. The key is to have easy access to your list, ensuring that it is readily available wherever you go.

Compiling a comprehensive list of your tasks serves several purposes:

- Mental clarity: Writing down your tasks helps offload the mental burden of trying to remember everything. This act alone creates space in your mind, reducing overwhelm.

- Organization and efficiency: A well-structured list will allow you to organize your tasks effectively. You can categorize them, set priorities, and establish timelines, making it easier to approach them in a systematic and efficient manner.

- Goal orientation: By listing the tasks necessary to accomplish your goals, you gain a clearer perspective on what needs to be done. This sense of direction empowers you to stay focused and work towards your objectives more effectively.

As you tackle the tasks on your list, you experience a sense of accomplishment with each completion, which can further boost your motivation and productivity. Tasks may change or evolve over time, and that is perfectly normal. Regularly review and update your lists to reflect your shifting priorities and goals accurately.

Minimizing Interruptions and Creating Mental Space

Sometimes, the most effective way to declutter your mind and achieve mental clarity is by addressing the interruptions that disrupt your workflow. In today's fast-paced and interconnected world, numerous distractions can impede your ability to focus and accomplish tasks. Identifying and managing these interruptions is crucial for boosting productivity and regaining control over your thoughts.

Take a moment to reflect on the potential interruptions you frequently encounter throughout the day. These may include:

- Smartphone notifications: Constant email, social media, and app notifications can be major disruptors. Instead of reacting to every ping, consider silencing non-essential notifications and designate specific times to check and respond to emails and messages.

- Office interruptions: Chatty coworkers or employees dropping by your office can break your concentration. To create a focused work environment, close your office door when necessary and use a "do not disturb" sign to signal your need for uninterrupted time.

- Multitasking: Constantly switching between tasks can hinder your ability to concentrate effectively. Avoid juggling multiple tasks at once and strive to complete one task before moving on to the next.

- Meetings and impromptu discussions: While collaboration is essential, excessive, and unproductive meetings or spontaneous discussions can disrupt your workflow. Consider scheduling focused work blocks and setting aside specific times for meetings.

- Social media and internet browsing: Aimless scrolling through social media feeds or browsing the internet can consume valuable time and clutter your mind. Set boundaries for internet usage during work hours and use website blockers if necessary.

Once you have identified potential interruptions, develop strategies to address them:

- Prioritize tasks: List your essential tasks and allocate specific time blocks for completing them. This structured approach helps you stay focused and minimizes distractions.

- Time management: Use time management techniques, such as the Pomodoro Technique, to work in focused intervals with short breaks in between. This method can improve productivity and concentration.

- Set boundaries: Communicate your need for uninterrupted focus to colleagues and family members, so they understand your designated work periods and respect your time.

- Optimize your workspace: Organize your workspace to minimize distractions. Keep essential tools and materials within reach and eliminate unnecessary clutter.

- Mindful technology use: Be intentional about how you use technology. Use apps or tools that block distractions during work hours and set specific times for personal technology usage.

Overcoming Procrastination and Unlocking Productivity

In our fast-paced lives, it is all too common to succumb to the temptation of procrastination. With numerous responsibilities and distractions vying for our attention, it is easy to put off tasks until the last minute. However, if we allow laziness or a lack of motivation to dictate our actions, we risk accumulating mental clutter that hampers our progress.

Fortunately, there are effective strategies to overcome procrastination and unlock our true productivity potential.
The simple truth is that completing the tasks on our plate is beneficial for our minds.

When we neglect our obligations and postpone necessary actions, they remain in the forefront of our thoughts, occupying valuable mental space. To combat procrastination, let us investigate the power of the two-minute rule and explore techniques to declutter our minds and achieve lasting success.

The two-minute rule serves as a powerful tool in overcoming procrastination. By asking ourselves, "What actions can I take in two minutes or less to move forward?"

We break down daunting tasks into manageable steps. When we commit to investing just two minutes into an assignment, we often find ourselves naturally inclined to continue working until the task is completed in its entirety.

This phenomenon, known as the Zeigarnik effect, highlights how unfinished tasks tend to linger in our memory, creating mental loops and hindering our overall clarity.

It is essential to recognize that even small actions are meaningful actions. By devoting a mere two minutes to a task, we initiate progress and disrupt the cycle of procrastination. As we build momentum and experience the satisfaction of completing even minor actions, we strengthen our resolve and motivate ourselves to tackle larger, more complex tasks.

While you may not resonate with every aspect of mental clutter discussed in this book, chances are you can relate to at least one area. If a particular strategy or tip resonates with you more than others, consider implementing it into your daily routine before exploring further.

Each step taken towards decluttering your mind contributes to enhanced mental clarity and paves the way for greater success in your professional endeavors.

There are no rigid rules when it comes to adopting these strategies. Feel free to experiment, adapt, and customize them to suit your unique preferences and circumstances.

Personalize your approach to maximizing productivity and reclaiming control over your thoughts. By finding effective ways to eliminate mental clutter, you pave the path to mental clarity and unlock your full potential for success in your personal and professional life.

Conclusion

In this transformative journey towards mental clarity, we have explored the profound impact of mental clutter on our lives and businesses. It is a universal issue that often goes unnoticed, but its consequences are far-reaching. Mental clutter robs us of the focus and energy we need to accomplish our goals and thrive in our endeavors.

The first step in overcoming mental clutter is recognition. By acknowledging its presence and understanding its effects, we lay the foundation for change.

As we dove into the various aspects of mental clutter, we learned that decluttering our minds is not an overnight process. It requires patience, dedication, and a commitment to self-improvement.

Starting small is the key. Identifying a specific area of our minds to work on and implementing the tactics presented in this book allows us to take the first steps towards mental clarity. Whether it is decluttering our physical environment, embracing mindfulness techniques, journaling our thoughts, or harnessing the power of physical exercise, every small effort counts.

In this pursuit of clarity, it is essential to be realistic with ourselves. The journey may present challenges and setbacks, but we must remain steadfast in our commitment to change. Celebrate the small victories along the way, as they mark progress towards a clearer mind and a more successful life.

As we come to the end of this book, I encourage you to reflect on the wisdom shared here and consider how you can apply these strategies to your life and business. The change you seek will not happen overnight, but with persistence and a dedication to self-improvement, you can pave the way for mental clarity and unleash your true potential.

Remember, mental clarity is not a destination but a continuous journey. Embrace it with an open mind, and you will discover newfound success and fulfillment in both your personal and professional endeavors. May this book serve as a guiding light on your path to a clutter-free and successful life.

Thank you for joining me on this exploration of mental clarity and its role in achieving greater success. Here is to a future filled with clarity, growth, and accomplishment.

Made in United States
Orlando, FL
11 September 2023